The Last Inn

Roshan B. Karki

ISBN: 9798844007224

DEDICATION

To my wife Roshina

You are parvati of my dreams

CONTENTS

ACKNOWLEDGMENTS

POEMS ABOUT SHIVA (GOD OF DEATH)

A Portrait of Shiva

So the mother hanged
picture of a Shiva
in a wooden frame
on her daughter's room.
Perhaps she did it so
thinking Shiva will protect her
or she will go doing
great things like Shiva
or she will get husband
like Shiva.

Look at the crescent moon.
With every new moon
the daughter is getting
more beautiful

The Shiva is ready to
fulfill her desire
to live beautifully.

And some day,
I am happy to say
she will get husband like Shiva.

At a Discotheque

I met you at a discotheque
where Death was DJ
and each day
he played a tune for us.

He played us song
of happiness and sorrow.
And we danced to his beat
but we were afraid of
his presence.

And each day we were
in love with his tunes.
He sang us folklore
of seas and sand dunes.

He had a mixer of time.
Out of his tunes
he made moon glitter
and star shine

Beware! The DJ knows where other world lies

Boons of Shiva

War is in my blood.
Shiva is in my faith.
He is so wonderful
even if he is god of death.
I will do great things to the world
because I have boons of Shiva.

Each day I pray
to the Lord meditating.
In Kailas Mountain he lays.
I am invincible as people say
I will erase hunger and famine.
Cause I have boons of Shiva.

Divine Weapons of Shiva

Lord Shiva can vanish and appear
from anyplace to anyplace he likes.
Shiva can sprinkle waters and cast spells
and make the dead the living once again.

His trisul can crack anything
even diamonds.
He can take impurity and
give purity.

His singles arrow
can mass destruct like missiles.
His single arrow
casted with spells
can kill thousands of men.

His chariot driven
by horses of death
can destroy any evils.
He can create weapons on his hand
chanting spells.

Gratitude (Based on law of attraction)

He is crying alone on pavements.
The lord came and asked him, "What are you grateful for?"
He said, "I have not eaten for days. I am grateful for breads."
The lord gave him bread factory.

Alone she is crying on pavement
waiting for her long lost love.
The lord asked, "What are you grateful for? "
She said, "Few seconds of happiness with my love."
The lord made her love come to her.

And I am sitting on room
preparing for exams at late night.
The lord came and asked, "What are you grateful for? "
I said, "I am grateful for divine visions."
He gave me visions of Shiva.

And I asked the lords, "What are you grateful for? "
He said, "I am grateful for helping with your lives."

Lord Shiva

You are meditating
on Kailas mountain and
you are controlling the world with third eye.
Crescent moon is your ornament.
Purity comes from your fountain.

The cobra is hissing as
a sign of kundalini rising.
Soon you will feel bliss
of stars and crescent moon shining.

Your clothes are made of tiger skin.
And damuri is your plaything.
You dance in your cosmic form Nat raja.
Dance Shiva. I can sing

Parvati is beautiful
and you are a wonderful being.
You guard the earth
and the world is your plaything.

My Horse of Death

Alexander the Great had Buchephalus.
My horse is named Adelius.
It can charge through any enemy lines.
I am King of the Battle and he is my lion.

It is black is color and has piercings on nose.
At night it breathes fire from lungs to its nose.
My horse is not afraid of death
because it is a carrier of Death itself.

It can understand the directions through telepathy.
Its saddle is silver
and rope is made of silk.
It can travel feet's in eye's blink.

My horse has given me numerous wins
and I owe it my life.
It's a loyal thing.
My hose of death will never die because
it represents death itself.

Riding on the Horse of Death

My horse is clever and cunning
As we trot down the valley
I am the head commander
Lord Shiva is in my faith
I am a part of him
I am God of death

The infantry follows me
Make no mistake. Act with haste
Let the sword dazzle and confuse enemies
At any cost we will have victory
For I am a part of Lord Shiva
I am god of death.

Riding with Shiva's Army

So the monsters
good and loyal to Shiva,
the vultures
Looking for food
evil in nature,
Black horses carrying death,
His army with horns
carrying spears with thorns,
are rushing
to erase evil.
Beware! I am riding Shiva's army

Lord Shiva on mountains is
controlling the war with third eye.
And I am using divine weapons
he gave me as gifts.
Beware! I am riding Shiva's army

Visions of Shiva

There is a door
and when you travel
through it,
you will enter a different room
with a different door.

Some will go to deep eternal sleep.
Some will go to different form of life.
The cycle depends on your spirituality
and Shiva manages all of it.

The reality is a
dream of Shiva.
Some say he is a weirdo
who needs nothing
but his visions and his Parvati.

Good will always
Win over evil.
Death rides with the good
as a chariot driver.
The good has Shiva's blessings.
And Shiva control s the world with his visions.

Lord Shiva! Let me serve you
Let me erase hunger and poverty.
God of death can give you life.
Let me do good things to the world
and only your grace can do that.

With your Grace

Let the rain come
and fall as tears.
Love is heaven and
it has several layers.

Tonight Shiva will
see us in his third eye.
He is meditating.
We both know where heaven lies.

Lord Shiva you are a wonderful being and
in your grace we dance and sing.

POEMS ABOUT MYTHICAL SUBJECTS

Angel with Broken Wings

The night was bright with full moon.
I was travelling across the woods.
And it was time to be midnight soon.
I hear something sob in the woods.

It must be a ghost or demon I thought.
But the crying was human
so I decided to look at it.
There was an angel with broken wings.

She had white wings with white feathers.
She was shy and was a wounded creature.
There was a glow in her face like candlesticks.
She was vomiting and she was sick.

I took her to my home and nursed her.
She then slept like moon under stars.
As days passes she was healed.
She told me tales of true fairy tales and treasures among the stars.

Now she is gone and she is my metaphor.
She is my bird of paradise and my faith.
Someday in the days I will join her.
Fairy tales are true if you think they are.

Crows in the Sky

A black bird
messenger to heaven
casts shadow
which is black like itself

A black bird
rules the sky
with its darkness
like a tether kite

Myth has it

Myth has it
Myth has it
It has my name
associated with
dragons and unicorns

Myth has it
Myth has it
Sinbad and Hercules
Footprints I have walked
And woods I have marked

Myth has it

Time to Heal

Give me time to heal
for I feel I have been wounded.
Shed a tears on my wounds like a unicorn
you heal it and I will begin again.

Are wounds parts of life?
It must be. So the god made unicorns
to heal the wounds
of people like me.

And I create wonders
if I being again
And the unicorn
will let me ride on his back once again.

POEMS ABOUT SOCIETY AND POLITCS

A New Dawn

Slowly the hour has hit midnight.
The demons from hell will come out alive.
But the time never remains the same.
The clock will hit new dawn soon.

Let children dream and wake up.
The stars will glitter and the moon will be here.
The God from heaven will save our dreams.
The clock will hit new dawn soon.

Let there be love and people make merry.
Don't be tired of waiting we are in pairs already.
The clock will hit midnight soon.
Cause it will be a new dawn soon.

There will be horizon and shooting stars.
Lovers will kiss and drink wine in bars.
Don't you go to sleep this night cause
there will be a new dawn tomorrow soon.

Hope

I have seen what hope is like
when you glance the world
through wet window panes
and the rain outside heals you.

I have seen what hope is like
when your pockets are empty
and you want to settle well
riding on a roll Royce.

I have seen what hope is like
when you write rhymes after rhymes
and your hope is to give hope to the world.

Myth to me

The world is a myth to me.
Enigmatic eyes let me see
you and your wonders.
The sky is in pain and in thunders.
The stars above are silent and sober.
And I am in my tent
dreaming dreams and wondering
no mortals dared to dream before.

Here in my barrack it is snowing
as if God gave a wrath.
The lord above is graceful and all knowing.
He is only person who knows clearly
what the world is doing.

Right now I am hero to world!
Honored be the Achilles and his legend.

And I will join the world
as a myth and as a hero.
Cause the lord above is graceful and all knowing.
But the worlds is a myth to me.

Riches and Poverty

I have seen what poverty is like.
When you eat soup with porridge and
the mother is confused
what she will feed her children
next day. There is no future here.
There is poverty but there is love.

Some say the best things in life and free.
The fruits are in the garden and you climb a tree.
Second best things are very expensive.
I have seen diamond rings glitter in your fingers.
I have slept in lavish palaces
where the marble have covered the floor
and the bedrooms are coated with gold.
I have drunk finest wine
and married to most powerful and beautiful woman.
But here is future and both love.

If live is living and having experiences
I have lived in both poverty and riches.

Tonight

Tonight,
the angels will be on sky.
The sun will glitter and the moon will shine.
Ghost riders will be on sky.
The dragon will burn the stones.
Mermaids will appear on sea bed.

Tonight,
the soldiers will go to war.
Preachers will preach.
Birds will chirp.
We will drink wine in bar.

And it can all happen.
It all can happen tonight.
There can be a fairytale world.
Moral values will be re sown.
There can be peace and development.

And it can all happen
if you ask the night.
It can all happen tonight.

War is over

Let's be brothers and
hold each other's arms.
Let the night be fun
Let soldiers take a break.
War is over if you want it.

Let us all listen folk tunes.
We are all human beings after all.
Let children dream
and let us save their dream.
War is over if you want it.

Youth and Politics

When you are young
you already are a small politician
as you have to draft your future.
You have to deal with schools and lectures.
There will be beautiful girls in class.
You should be a little hot.
You should be a little cool.

The teachers teach you
to be a good citizen.
School is your parliament
and books are your oxygen.

And someday you will walk the planet
with goodness and justice.
Because when you are young
you already are a small politician.

POEMS ABOUT EVENTS AND PLACES

A Step Ahead

Dare to move forward
because a step ahead
victory lies
and freedom lies

You and I have both
walked hundreds of miles.
Travel a step ahead because
here the victory lies.

Let the last step be with
Freedom and courage.
Let it be a legacy.
Let's move a step ahead.

Compose you a song

Bring the guitar in different tune
and let it sound
like a howl.
Let me compose you a song.

I got my own chords.
I got my own scales.
To your ears it will sound magnificent.
The guitar is in different tune.

I will take inspiration
from your kiss.
Creativity is wonderful,
talent is bliss.
I will compose you a song
you have never heard of.

And it will be played
across the world
in amphitheatres.
Let me compose you a song '
you never heard of
because my guitar is in different tune.

Kathmandu in Nights

The city shimmers like stars in sky.
Here between the two great countries Aryan civilization lies.
You will feel the rhythm of culture
when you walk at streets of Kathmandu in Nights.

Some part of town lies awake in night
Under the stars the concrete houses are asleep.
The bell in Ghanta Ghar is ringing.
The new road is colorful
when you walk along the streets in Kathmandu at nights.

The Last Inn

Hello passengers!
You must be tired.
Are you hungry?
It must be long road
from your home.
The sky above has thunder.
We got fresh soup to serve.
Eat it or not
it's your last chance
because you are at the last inn
on the highway.

May be you want a pint of beer.
The weather is perfect for some liquor.
You get warm with feelings.
Because when you wake up tomorrow
you got a long way to go.
The maid is beautiful
and she will serve you.
Drink it or not
it's your last chance
because you are at the last inn on highway

The lights are dim.
So is the moon.
The passengers are quiet.
Welcome to the last inn on highway.

Winter Moon

There is no light here.
The moon is hiding behind the clouds.
The creatures are hibernating.
Welcome the winter moon.

You are I are safe
inside our huts
looking through the window
drinking tea

But the moon
pale and yellow
is hiding
in its own world

The nights are cold
Will the moon feel it?
I deny it.
Welcome the winter moon.

POEMS ABOUT LOVE

Almighty lovers

Like always,
I will wait for you at park
in rain or in thunder.
You make me wonder with
your hazel black eyes which
reminds me of skies.
Our love is like almighty Himalayas.
That cannot be bought
neither can it be sold

Even the most deadly
poison won't affect us.
I will hold your hands
in rain and thunder
even in bars on clubs
We will be almighty lovers.

Buy Love in Stores

I have searched for you in broken pavements.
There were cracks but it was adventurous.
There were numerous footprints and
these must be of people like me I thought.

So there were rotten roses
defrosted and decayed like plants in snow.
And I passed a church
where people pray and bow
Looking for their lovers.

Few decades and we will get old.
Come stay with and make me feel bold.
Some say the lord sold this world to lovers.
You can buy love fresh in fresh by stores.

Feel a Paradise

Your siren eyes
know where heaven lies.
Your eyes know
Constellations and zodiacs.
You make me feel
like a paradise.

Your hair soft
as silk
glitters in sun rays.
You belong to me.
Let the star glitter
and moon shine.
You make me feel
like a paradise.

Go Mad in Love with you

I want to ignore the world.
I want to do something bold.
I want to go mad in love with you
as you are my greatest treasures

The sun and the moon is shining for us
We will go on a road trip to heaven on a bus.
We will see both heaven and angels.
Let me submit my life you.
Let me go mad in love with you.

Roshina, my sweetheart
let me go mad in love
and quench my thirst
and fulfill life's purpose.

How the Days are passing

I do not know how the days are passing.
Are they passing swiftly like wind or white like snow.
We are both travelling along the road.
We will be better together that's one thing I know.

Do other travelers feel the same I wonder?
The moon is silent and sky has thunder.
It will be difficult alone but we will face it.
With your presence the beacons on the way will be lit

I will hold your hands and we will go on a voyage.
You be my lover and I do not mind being a sage.
Cause I do not know how days are passing.
But with you every day will be a magical delight.

I have loved you

I have loved you
with all my heart
like no one else
Soulfully,
Like Shiva to Parvati
Every day is a routine,
an excuse
to be together with you.
Each hour I feel eternal
like stars in the sky.
Each day I feel glad
like the moon.

Our love like
a drink of wine
goes to the sea.

Let me love you
because I have loved you
like nobody else.

In Your Arms Mother

Today is the day
we are finally together.
I finally got to meet you.
Hold me in your arms mother.
Make me feel warm.

I have been waiting for this moment
since years and it will be another soon.
Hold me in your arms mother.
Make me feel warm.

Your affection guarded me.
I have finally met you.
Hold me in your arms mother.
Make me feel warm.

Life and Sunsets

Let life be a day
The sunrise be the birth
The sunset be the death
The night is time
To kiss your lover.
The day is time
to work and wonder.

Don't you miss me
if my eyes
miss the sunsets.
Cause you gave my life
a meaning in cold nights.
Tea and your smile
made my every day.
I will be waiting for you
beyond the sun
where we will lay
where the paradise lays.

Make me Invincible tonight

If the whole world stands against you
I will hold your hand and fight with you.
Let us be together this night.
Make me invincible tonight.

Tomorrow there are wars to be won
and there are things to be done.
Ignore all of them tonight.
Make me invincible this night.

Kiss me as I am the boldest knight.
Let us our body be full of light.
Let me conquer your body tonight.
Because tomorrow when we wake up
there are wars to be won and things to be done.

My Wonder woman

Oh! My woman
My clever woman
My wonder woman
Romantic yet modest
One among the best
Kiss me! Do not act in haste
Let me feel every inch of you
We are two doves in a nest
Peaceful yet iconic
When I touch you
I feel I am living pentatonic scales
You must feel the same
The moon is silent and lame
We are burning for some riches
Also some fame
Only love exists in our nest
The forest is good place to make love
The forest is with love and peace.

POEMS ABOUT ME

A Captain to the Ship

Let there be light
on black and cold nights.
The stars are here
The moon is on sight

The ship is on horizon.
will it sink or sail?
It is carrying whole world
as brothers as tales untold.

The captain is drunk and asleep
with a bottle of merlot.
Bu t the ship soon
will hit the port.

He is dreaming dreams
No mortals dared to dream before.
Should I wake him or let him sleep?
I am in deep trouble. It's four am.

The ship may crash.
We are together at last and
wet are my eye lashes.
Let the captain sleep
I will guide the ship.

Let me be captain to the ship!

A Dreamer

I am no one but a dreamer.
The sky is silent the moon is paler.
I am with light, right.
I am with changes that are at my sight.

I am no one but a dreamer.
Dreaming is a special force.
Let me come out of the wooden door.
I am no one but a dreamer.

As I write Poetry

As I write poems where
metaphors are my seas
simile is my sun
and my visions are the moon.

I feel I am more spiritual
with each rhymes.
I feel alive and smart.
My copy knows it.

Every day is an agenda
to write a poem a day.
The man is a great surrealist
let people say

It cleans my heart
and unleashes my soul.
I submit my work to heaven.
I submit my work to Gods.

Know my name

Hey stranger do you know my name?
Cause I have been working so hard
to go on stage and to create a page
with other legend.

The horizon wants me
and I work so hard
pressing piano keys and writing lyrics.
I want to be the chosen one.
The eagles are chirping on horizon.
Hey stranger do you know my name?

Let's do Something

Will love conquer the world?
I think it can.
It can quench thirst of my soul
and give meaning to my life.

Let's kiss and make merry.
We will create a wonderful story.
You and I are on stage and
each day is a page we can turn to.

Let's do something.

Night full of Rain

The moon is hiding
beyond the clouds.
Here come the night again.
The sky is crying. The night is full of rain.

But I cannot hear your whispers
The sky is in thunder and in anger.
The nymphs at bottom of sea do not know it.
Here come the night with rain once again.

But the night with rain
is perfect place to make love.
The moon defines a lover's identity.
Welcome the night full of rain.

Poetry is Magic

The words float on paper
like distant clouds on the sky.
Poetry can heal the wounded and lepers.
I write about heaven and where it lies.

And when you read my poems
you will feel healed.
Poetry is magic.
I am a magician

Let me cast a spell on you.

Tales not told

I believe in fighting for what I believe in.
I have tales to tell the world has seldom seen.
I have a gentle heart and I am a human being.
I believe in fighting for good and my heart is clean.

Let us do wonder in the world.
Let us create tales no one has told.
One third of my life is gone and remaining is twofold.
But the moon is silent the stars are cold.

Thorns on the Way

I know what thorns are.
I have stepped on them
and walked until my feet bled
and there was no option
other then keep walking.

And still there are thorns.
They will never go away.
I have learned to walk on thorns.

But you have changed my way.
You lead me to a better path
where there are no thorns but
there are magic and dreams.

Up in the Skies

Let me go up in the skies
with my dream airplane.
I know where the heave lies.
The plane is painted with my name.

High up we will go
the sky has no boundaries.
We will look down below
at houses and tall trees.

We will see the seas.
We will see the deserts.
You and I will fly
up high in the sky.

Writing Poems

Writing poems are relaxing
when I plant a thought
after a day's hard work and
the words come out god on page.

It's my mini movies.
It's my survival instinct.
The words will bear fruit
after a day's hard work.

ABOUT THE AUTHOR

Roshan B. Karki (Roshan Bikram Kark) is a poet, writer, musician, entrepreneur and politician. He was born in Charikot, Dolkha. He has attended Loras College, USA as a honors student to pursue undergraduate in Creative writing. " The Last Inn" is seventeenth book by the author. It consists of themes of love, life, events, supernatural powers with major theme of god of death in eastern mysticism known as Shiva.

www.ingramcontent.com/pod-product-compliance
Lightning Source LLC
La Vergne TN
LVHW041251150826
845673LV00008B/2536

* 9 7 9 8 8 4 4 0 0 7 2 2 4 *